SCHOLASTIC
**News**
Nonfiction Readers

# Windy Weather Days

## by Katie Marsico

Children's Press®
A Division of Scholastic Inc.
New York  Toronto  London  Auckland  Sydney
Mexico City  New Delhi  Hong Kong
Danbury, Connecticut

These content vocabulary word builders are for grades 1–2.
Subject Consultants: Robert Van Winkle, Chief Meteorologist, WBBH, Fort Myers, Florida; and Jack Williams, Public Outreach Coordinator, American Meteorological Society, Boston, Massachusetts

Reading Consultant: Cecilia Minden-Cupp, PhD, Former Director, Language and Literacy Program, Harvard Graduate School of Education, Cambridge, Massachusetts

Photographs © 2007: Corbis Images: 4 top, 17 (Tom Bean), 9 (Peter M. Fisher), 20 top (Walter Geiersperger), 21 bottom (W. Geiersperger), back cover, 5 top right, 13 inset (Japack Company), 20 bottom (Joson/zefa), 2, 5 bottom right, 15 (Matthias Kulka), 5 top left, 12 (NASA), 23 bottom right (Royalty-Free), 21 top (Sidney/zefa), cover, 19 (Ariel Skelley), 23 bottom left (Jim Sugar), 11 (Craig Tuttle), 4 bottom right (A & J Verkaik); Index Stock Imagery: 13 (AbleStock), 23 top right (photolibrary. com pty. ltd.), 4 bottom left, 10 (Mick Roessler), 23 top left (ThinkStock LLC); Photo Researchers, NY/ Richard Hutchings: 1, 5 bottom left, 7.

Book Design: Simonsays Design!
Book Production: The Design Lab

Library of Congress Cataloging-in-Publication Data

Marsico, Katie, 1980–
 Windy weather days / Katie Marsico.
   p. cm. — (Scholastic news nonfiction readers)
 Includes index.
 ISBN-10: 0-531-16774-7
 ISBN-13: 978-0-531-16774-8
 1. Winds—Juvenile literature. I. Title. II. Series.
 QC931.4.T78 2007
 551.51'8—dc22                          2006013309

1 2 3 4 5 6 7 8 9 10 R 16 15 14 13 12 11 10 09 08 07

# CONTENTS

# WORD HUNT

Look for these words as you read. They will be in **bold**.

**clouds**
(kloudz)

**snowflakes**
(**snoh**-flayks)

**thunderstorm**
(**thuhn**-dur-storm)

4

**Earth**
(urth)

**seeds**
(seeds)

**wind**
(wind)

**wind sock**
(wind sohk)

# A Windy Day

Tree branches sway back and forth, and leaves blow across the street. You better hang onto your hat!

The wind is blowing today.

The word *wind* means "to blow."

In the spring, the wind pushes puffy rain **clouds** overhead. It gently blows bright, colorful flowers back and forth.

In the summer, the wind moves white clouds across a clear, blue sky. It cools your face when the weather is hot.

The wind pushes puffy, white clouds on a bright summer day.

In the fall, the wind shakes red, yellow, and orange leaves from the treetops.

In the winter, the wind makes **snowflakes** swirl in the air.

**snowflakes**

How do these colorful leaves end up on the ground? Wind blows them off the trees!

So, what is wind? Wind is air that's moving. It is found everywhere on Earth.

Wind helps to warm and cool **Earth**.

It blows dirt and **seeds** across the land.

**Earth**

**Wind blows dirt and seeds that help trees, plants, and flowers grow.**

seeds

Have you ever seen a wind sock? Wind fills a wind sock.

The **wind sock** shows which direction the wind is coming from. It also helps people see how hard the wind is blowing.

**Wind socks show how strong the wind is.**

Some wind can be very strong. Strong winds spin inside a **thunderstorm**.

Other wind is no more than a gentle breeze that brushes past your face.

**Thunderstorms usually happen in spring and summer.**

The next time the wind blows, try sailing a boat or flying a kite. Or just hang onto your hat and watch the leaves gather at your feet.

# WHAT ELSE CAN YOU DO ON A WINDY DAY?

You can visit a wind farm! A wind farm uses the wind to help make electricity.

Wind farms have special machines called windmills.

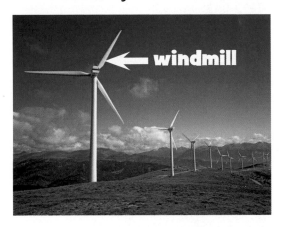

windmill

Windmills are tall and look like they have large, long arms coming out of their tops.

The wind blows, and the arms on the windmill spin.

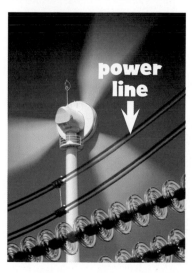

power line

The windmills are connected to machines that make electricity. The electricity flows off the farm through large wires called power lines.

# YOUR NEW WORDS

**clouds** (kloudz) white or gray masses that float in the sky and are made up of water and ice

**Earth** (urth) the planet on which we live

**seeds** (seeds) the parts of a plant from which new plants can grow

**snowflakes** (**snoh**-flayks) single pieces, or flakes, of snow

**thunderstorm** (**thuhn**-dur-storm) a storm that happens when ice and water rub together inside a cloud

**wind** (wind) air that is moving

**wind sock** (wind sohk) a piece of cloth that the wind blows through and that is used to show the strength and direction of the wind

# FUN THINGS YOU MIGHT SEE BLOWING IN THE WIND

**pinwheel**

**toy sailboat**

**weather vane**

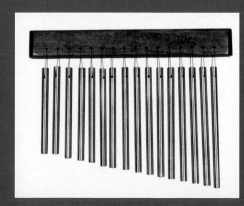

**wind chimes**

23

# INDEX

## FIND OUT MORE
**Book:**
Parker, Steve. *Wind Power*. Milwaukee: Gareth Stevens Publishing, 2004.

**Website:**
Weather Wiz Kids: Wind
http://www.weatherwizkids.com/wind1.htm

## MEET THE AUTHOR:
Katie Marsico is a freelance writer and editor who lives with her family in Chicago, Illinois. Katie loves windy days—especially when she's snug in her bed with a good book to read!